BITE-SIZE
BEN FRANKLIN

ALSO BY JOHN P. HOLMS AND KARIN BAJI

Bite-Size Twain
Bite-Size Lincoln

BITE-SIZE
BEN FRANKLIN

Wit & Wisdom from
a Founding Father

COMPILED BY JOHN P. HOLMS AND KARIN BAJI

ST. MARTIN'S PRESS ⚞ NEW YORK

THOMAS DUNNE BOOKS.
An imprint of St. Martin's Press.

Library of Congress Cataloging-in-Publication Data

Franklin, Benjamin, 1706–1790.
    Bite-size Franklin : wit & wisdom from a founding father /
John P. Holms and Karin Baji, compilers.
       p. cm.
    "Thomas Dunne books."
    ISBN 0-312-19835-3
    1. Franklin, Benjamin, 1706–1790—Quotations.
2. Quotations, American.   3. Maxims, American.   I. Holms,
John P., 1944– . II. Baji, Karin. III. Title.
E302.F83   1999
973.3'092—dc21   98–47388
                                          CIP

10 9 8 7 6 5 4 3 2

Contents

Preface xi

FRANKLIN ON FRANKLIN 1

ON AGING 3

ON AMERICA & ITS PROMISE 6

ON ANGER 7

ON ART & MUSIC 8

ON AVARICE 9

ON BEAUTY 11

ON BLAME & PRESUMPTION 12

ON CLOTHES 13

ON COLONIAL GRIEVANCES & FOOD FOR REBELLION . . .14

ON DEATH & THE HEREAFTER 17

ON DEBT & DEBTORS 18

ON DOCTORS 20

ON DRINK 20

ON EDUCATION & HIGHER LEARNING 22

ON FAITH, RELIGION, & ENLIGHTENMENT 25

ON FAME 29

ON FOOD & APPETITE 31

ON FOOLS & FOLLIES 32

ON FRIENDS & FOES .32

ON GEORGE WASHINGTON 36

ON GIFTS & INGRATITUDE 36

ON HOUSEGUESTS .37

ON HOW TO SUCCEED IN LIFE 38

ON HUMAN ERROR .42

ON INDUSTRY & MERIT 43

ON JUSTICE & THE COURTS 46

ON LAWYERS 47

ON LIBERTY 47

ON LOVE & MARRIAGE 49

ON MONEY 52

ON OPINIONS 53

ON PASSIONS & PLEASURES 54

ON A PENNY SAVED 56

ON PEOPLE IN GENERAL 57

ON THE ART OF PERSUASION 59

ON POVERTY & RICHES 60

ON PRIDE & SELF-WORTH 62

ON PRINCIPLES OF GOVERNMENT 65

ON PUBLIC OFFICE 67

ON SCIENTIFIC EXPERIMENT 69

ON "SOCIETY" 72

ON TIME 74

ON TOO MUCH TALK 75

ON THE UNITED STATES CONSTITUTION 77

ON VIRTUE, THE GOOD LIFE, & A GOOD EXAMPLE 79

ON WAR, PEACE, & OUR READINESS FOR BOTH 81

Benjamin Franklin (1706–1790) 85

PREFACE

Courteous Reader,

I have heard that nothing gives an author so great
pleasure as to find his works respectfully quoted
by other learned authors. This pleasure I have seldom enjoyed; for though I have been, if I may say
it without vanity, an eminent author of almanacs
annually now a full quarter of a century, my
brother authors in the same way, for what reason
I know not, have ever been very sparing in their
applauses, and no other author has taken the least
notice of me, so that did not my writings produce
me some solid pudding, the great deficiency of
praise would have quite discouraged me.

I concluded at length that the people were
the best judges of my merit, for they buy my
works; and besides, in my rambles, where I am
not personally known, I have frequently heard
one or other of my adages repeated, with "as Poor
Richard says," at the end on it. . . .

I found [a] good man had thoroughly stud-
ied my Almanacs, and digested all I had dropped
on these topics during the course of five and
twenty years. The frequent mention he made of
me must have tired anyone else, but my vanity

was wonderfully delighted with it, though I was conscious that not a tenth part of the wisdom was my own, which he ascribed to me, but rather the gleanings I had made of the sense of all ages and nations. However, I resolved to be the better for the echo of it; and though I had at first determined to buy stuff for a new coat, I went away resolved to wear my old one a little longer. Reader, if thou wilt do the same, thy profit will be as great as mine. I am, as ever, thine to serve thee,

July 7, 1757

—Poor Richard Improved, 1758

ACKNOWLEDGMENTS

WE'D LIKE TO THANK TOM, PETE, KRISTEN, MATT AND ALL THE REST AT ST. MARTIN'S FOR THEIR SUPPORT AND HARD WORK. AND EACH OTHER FOR A PARTNERSHIP THAT YIELDS MUCH BEYOND WORDS. ALSO, AS USUAL, WE THANK LEFTY, WHO DOESN'T KNOW WHAT A GREAT HELP HE IS.

Though I never arrived at the perfection I had been so ambitious of obtaining, but fell far short of it, yet I was, by the endeavor, a better and a happier man than I otherwise should have been if I had not attempted it.

—BENJAMIN FRANKLIN

FRANKLIN ON FRANKLIN

[Epitaph for himself composed in 1728, at age twenty-two]

> *The Body of*
> *Benjamin Franklin*
> *Printer*
> *(Like the cover of an old book,*
> *Its contents torn out*
> *And stripped of its lettering and gilding)*
> *Lies here, food for worms.*
> *But the work shall not be lost*
> *For it will (as he believed) appear once more*
> *In a new and more elegant edition*
> *Revised and Corrected*
> *By*
> *The Author.*

I grew tired of meekness when I saw it without effect. Of late therefore I have been saucy, and in two papers, *Rules for Reducing a Great Empire to a Small One;* and, *An Edict of the King of Prussia,* I have held up a looking glass in which some ministers may see their ugly faces, and their nation its injustice. Those papers have been much taken notice of, many are pleased with them and a few very angry, who I am told will make me feel their Resentment, which I must bear as well as I can, and shall bear the better if any public good is done.

[Writing from Paris] I know you wish you could see me; but, as you can't, I will describe myself to you. Figure me in your mind as jolly as formerly, and as strong and hearty, only a few years older; very plainly dressed, wearing my thin grey straight hair, that peeps out under my only *coiffure,* a fine fur cap, which comes down my forehead almost to my spectacles. Think how this must appear among the powdered heads of Paris!

I am very happy in being at home, where I am allowed to know when I have eat enough, and drink enough, am warm enough, and sit in a place that I like and no-body pretends to know what I feel better than I do myself.

You desire me to send you all the political pieces I have been the author of. I have never kept them. They were most of them written occasionally for transient purposes, and having done their business, they die and are forgotten. I could as easily make a collection for you of all the past parings of my nails.

I have now been upwards of 50 years employed in public offices. When I informed your good friend that I was ordered to France, being then 70 years old, and observed that the public, having as it were eaten my flesh, seemed now resolved to pick my bones, he replied that he approved their taste, for that the nearer the bone the sweeter the meat.

And now I speak of thanking God, I desire with all humility to acknowledge, that I owe the mentioned happiness of my past life to his kind providence, which led me to the means I used and gave them success.

On Aging

By my rambling digressions I perceive myself to be grown old.

All would live long, but none would be old.

At twenty years of age the will reigns; at thirty the wit; at forty the judgment.

Hot things, sharp things, sweet things, cold things
All rot the teeth, and make them look like old things.

Wish not so much to live long as to live well.

Many foxes grow grey, but few grow good.

An old young man will be a young old man.

Old boys have their playthings as well as young ones; the difference is only in the price.

The older I grow, the more apt I am to doubt my own judgment, and to pay more respect to the judgment of others.

Youth is pert and positive, Age modest and doubting: So ears of corn when young and light, stand bolt upright, but hang their heads when weighty, full, and ripe.

In every animal that walks upright the deficiency of the fluids that fill the muscles appears first in the highest part. The face first grows lank and wrinkled; then the neck; then the breast and arms; the lower parts continuing to the last as plump as ever.

Having their own way is one of the greatest comforts of life to old people. . . . When they have long lived in a house, it becomes natural to them; they are almost as closely connected with it as the tortoise with his shell; they die, if you tear them out of it; old folks and old trees, if you remove them, it is ten to one that you kill them.

I seem to have intruded myself into the company of posterity, when I ought to have been abed and asleep. Yet, had I gone at 70, it would have cut off twelve of the most active years of my life, employed too in matters of the greatest importance; and whether I have been doing good or mischief is for time to discover.

People who live long, who will drink of the cup of life to the very bottom, must expect to meet with some of the usual dregs; and when I reflect on the number of terrible maladies human nature is subject to, I think myself favored in having to my share only the stone and the gout.

> For my own personal ease I should have died two years ago; but, though those years have been spent in excruciating pain, I am pleased that I have lived them. . . . Whatever state of existence I am placed hereafter, if I retain any memory of

what has passed here, I shall with it retain the esteem, respect, and affection with which I have
long been, my dear friend, yours most sincerely,
B. Franklin

ON AMERICA & ITS PROMISE

America, where people do not inquire concerning a
stranger, "What is he?" but, "what can he do?"

In short, America is the land of labor, and by no means
what the English call Lubberland, and the French Pays
de Cocagne, where the streets are said to be paved with
half-peck loaves, the houses tiled with pancakes, and
where the fowls fly about ready roasted, crying, "Come
eat me!"

America, an immense territory, favored by nature with
all advantages of climate, soil, great navigable rivers,
and lakes, etc., must become a great country, populous
and mighty; and will, in less time than is generally con-
ceived, be able to shake off any shackles that may be im-
posed on her, and perhaps place them on the imposers.

I wish the bald eagle had not been chosen as the representative of our country; he is a bird of bad moral character; like those among men who live by sharping and robbing, he is generally poor, and often very lousy. The turkey is a much more respectable bird, and withal a true original native of America.

[Setting sail from England to return to America] I am going from the old world to the new, and I feel like those who are leaving this world for the next; grief at the parting, fear at the passage; hope of the future.

On Anger

Anger is never without a reason, but seldom with a good one.

> *Take this remark from Richard poor and lame,*
> *Whate'er's begun in anger ends in shame.*

Neglect kills injuries, revenge increases them.

'Tis more noble to forgive, and more manly to despise, than to revenge an injury.

Write injuries in dust, benefits in marble.

> *Doing an injury puts you below your enemy;*
> *Revenging one makes you but even with him;*
> *Forgiving it sets you above him.*

A quarrelsome man has no good neighbors.

He that blows the coals in quarrels he has nothing to do with has no right to complain if the sparks fly in his face.

A temper to bear much will have much to bear.

The too obliging temper is evermore disobliging itself.

Take heed of the vinegar of sweet wine, and the anger of good-nature.

Anger warms the invention, but overheats the oven.

On Art & Music

Paintings and fightings are best seen at a distance.

The pleasure which artists feel in hearing much of that composed in the modern taste is not the natural pleasure arising from melody or harmony of sounds, but of the same kind with the pleasure we feel on seeing the surprising feats of tumblers and rope dancers who execute difficult things.

[Praising a good Scottish tune] The connoisseurs in modern music will say I have no taste; but I cannot help adding that I believe our ancestors, in hearing a good song, distinctly articulated, sung to one of those tunes, and accompanied by the harp, felt more real pleasure than is communicated by the generality of modern operas, exclusive of that arising from the scenery and dancing.

How happy is he, who can . . . please his ear with any music, delight his eye with any painting, any sculpture, any architecture, and divert his mind with any book or any company! How many mortifications must he suffer, that cannot bear anything but beauty, order, elegance and perfection! Your man of taste, is nothing but a man of distaste.

ON AVARICE

Avarice and Happiness never saw each other, how then should they become acquainted.

He does not possess wealth, it possesses him.

Prosperity discovers vice, adversity virtue.

A rich rogue, is like a fat hog, who never does good till as dead as a log.

Pray don't burn my house to roast your eggs.

Success has ruined many a man.

If you desire many things, many things will seem but a few.

Many a man would have been worse, if his estate had been better.

Proportion your charity to the strength of your estate, or God will proportion your estate to the weakness of your charity.

If worldly goods cannot save me from death, they ought not to hinder me of eternal life.

If your riches are yours, why don't you take them with you to the other world?

Avarice and ambition are strong passions, and, separately, act with great force on the human mind; but, when both are united, and may be gratified in the same object, their violence is almost irresistible, and they hurry men headlong into factions and contentions, destructive of all good government.

Ambition often spends foolishly what avarice had wickedly collected.

On Beauty

Beauty and folly are old companions.

If Jack's in love, he's no judge of Jill's beauty.

Virtue may not always make a face handsome, but vice will certainly make it ugly.

Vice knows she's ugly, so puts on her mask.

On Blame & Presumption

The absent are never without fault, nor the present without excuse.

You may sometimes be much in the wrong, in owning your being in the right.

A benevolent man should allow a few faults in himself, to keep his friends in countenance.

He that is good for making excuses is seldom good for anything else.

Clean your Finger, before you point at my Spots.

Blame-all and Praise-all are two blockheads.

Approve not of him who commends all you say.

Don't throw stones at your neighbors', if your own windows are glass.

> *He that would live in peace and ease,*
> *Must not speak all he knows, nor judge all he sees.*

Presumption first blinds a man, then sets him a running.

Despair ruins some, presumption many.

Happy Tom Crump, ne'er sees his own hump.

Who has deceived thee so oft as thyself?

On Clothes

Eat to please thyself, but dress to please others.

The cat in gloves catches no mice.

Many a one, for the sake of finery on the back, has gone with a hungry belly, and half-starved their families. "Silks and satins, scarlets and velvets, put out the kitchen fire," as Poor Richard says.

Don't judge of men's wealth or piety, by their Sunday appearances.

He has lost his boots but saved his spurs.

The wolf sheds his coat once a year; his disposition, never,

> *Fond pride of dress is sure an empty curse;*
> *E'er fancy you consult, consult your purse.*

On Colonial Grievances & Food for Rebellion

There is in [America] scarce a man, there is not a single native of our country, who is not firmly attached to his king by principle and affection. But a new kind of loyalty seems to be required of us, a loyalty to Parliament; a loyalty that is to extend, it is said, to a surrender of all our properties, whenever a house of commons (in which there is not a single member of our choosing) shall think fit to grant them away without our consent.

There are natural duties which precede political ones and cannot be extinguished by them.

There cannot be a stronger natural right than that of a man's making the best profit he can of the natural produce of his lands.

And if, through increase of people, two smiths are wanted for one employed before, why may not the new smith be allowed to live and thrive in the new country, as well as the old in the old? In fine, why should the countenance of a state be partially afforded to its people, unless it be most in favor of those who have most merit? And if there be any difference, those who have most contributed to enlarge Britain's empire and commerce, increase her strength, her wealth, and the numbers of her people, at the risk of their own lives and private fortunes in new and strange countries, methinks ought rather to expect some preference.

Question: What used to be the pride of the Americans?
Answer: To indulge in the fashions and manufactures of Great Britain.

Question: What is now their pride?
Answer: To wear their old clothes over again, till they can make new ones.

Every man in England seems to consider himself as a piece of a sovereign over America; seems to jostle himself into the throne with the king, and talks of *our subjects in the colonies.*

Compelling the colonies to pay money without their consent would be rather like raising contributions in an enemy's country than taxing of Englishmen for their own public benefit.

People who have property in a country which they may lose, and privileges which they may endanger, are generally disposed to be quiet, and even to bear much, rather than to hazard all. While the government is mild and just, while important civil and religious rights are secure, such subjects will be dutiful and obedient. The waves do not rise but when the winds blow.

Idleness and pride tax with a heavier hand than kings and parliaments. If we can get rid of the former, we may easily bear the latter.

[At the signing of the Declaration of Independence, July 4, 1776] We must all hang together, or assuredly we shall all hang separately.

Rebellion against tyrants is obedience to God.

On Death & the Hereafter

Death takes no bribes.

A man is not completely born until he is dead. Why then should we grieve that a new child is born among the immortals, a new member added to their happy society?

Our friend and we are invited abroad on a party of pleasure, which is to last forever. His chair was ready first, and he is gone before us. We could not all conveniently start together; and why should you and I be grieved at this, since we are soon to follow, and know where to find him?

When I observe that there is great frugality, as well as wisdom, in His works, since He has been evidently sparing both of labor and materials; for by the various wonderful inventions of propagation, He has provided for the continual peopling of the world with plants and animals, without being at the trouble of repeated creations; and by the natural reduction of compound substances to their original elements, capable of being employed in new compositions, He has prevented the necessity of creating new matter. . . . When I see nothing annihilated, and not even a drop of water wasted, I cannot suspect the annihilation of souls, or believe, that he will suffer the daily waste of millions of minds ready made that now exist, and put himself to the continual trouble of making new ones. Thus finding myself to exist in the world, I believe I shall, in some shape or other, always exist.

On Debt & Debtors

When you run in debt, you give another power over your liberty.

What would you think of that prince, or that government, who should issue an edict forbidding you to dress like a gentleman or a gentlewoman, on pain of imprisonment or servitude? Would you not say, that you are free, have a right to dress as you please, and that such an edict would be a breach of your privileges, and such a government tyrannical? And yet you are about to put yourself under that tyranny when you run in debt for such dress!

The second vice is lying; the first is running in debt.

Debt is a prolific mother of folly and of crime.

Pay what you owe, and what you're worth you'll know.

'Tis against some men's principle to pay interest, and seems against others interest to pay the principal.

Remember that credit is money.

He's gone, and forgot nothing but to say farewell to his creditors.

The creditors are a superstitious sect, great observers of set days and times.

If you'd know the value of money, go try to borrow some; for he that goes a-borrowing goes a-sorrowing.

Lend money to an enemy, and thou'lt gain him; to a friend, and thou'lt lose him.

The borrower is a slave to the lender; the security to both.

Rather go to bed supperless than rise in debt.

On Doctors

He's the best physician that knows the worthlessness of most medicines.

God heals and the doctor takes the fee.

He's a fool that makes his doctor his heir.

Beware of the young doctor and the old barber.

It is ill jesting with the joiner's tools, worse with the doctor's.

I have, indeed, sometimes moderate fits of the gout; but I think it is not settled among the physicians whether that is a disease or a remedy.

There are more old drunkards than old doctors.

On Drink

Drink does not drown care, but waters it, and makes it grow faster.

Take counsel in wine, but resolve afterwards in water.

'Tis true, drinking does not improve our faculties, but it enables us to use them.

Much study and experience, and a little liquor, are of absolute necessity for some tempers . . . the moderate use of liquor and a well-placed and well-regulated anger often produce this same effect; and some who cannot ordinarily talk but in broken sentences and false grammar, do in the heat of passion express themselves with as much eloquence as warmth.

He that drinks fast, pays slow.

When the wine enters, out goes the truth.

> *Life with fools consists in drinking;*
> *With the wise man, living's thinking.*

Nothing more like a fool, than a drunken man.

I say this to you . . . like a good Christian . . . that the Apostle Paul very seriously advised Timothy to put some wine into his water for health's sake; but that not one of the apostles nor any of the holy fathers have ever recommended putting water into wine.

ON EDUCATION & HIGHER LEARNING

Genius without education is like silver in the mine.

Most of the learning in use, is of no great use.

Today is Yesterday's Pupil.

Those things that hurt, instruct.

Learn of the skillful: He that teaches himself hath a fool for his master.

Proud modern learning despises the ancient: Schoolmen are now laughed at by schoolboys.

Experience keeps a dear school, but fools will learn in no other.

The ancients tells us what is best; but we must learn of the moderns what is fittest.

Pillgarlic was in the accusative case, and bespoke a lawyer in the vocative, who could not understand him till he made use of the dative.

The learned fool writes his nonsense in better language than the unlearned; but still 'tis nonsense.

Tim was so learned that he could name a horse in nine languages. So ignorant, that he bought a cow to ride on.

The Temple of Learning: Every peasant, who had wherewithal, was preparing to send one of his children at least to this famous place; and in this case most of them consulted their own purses instead of their children's capacities. . . . Parents who, blind to their children's dullness, and insensible of the solidity of their skulls, because they think their purses can afford it, will send them to the Temple of Learning, where, for want of a suitable genius, they learn little more than how to carry themselves handsomely, and enter a room genteely . . . and from whence they return, after abundance of trouble and charge, as great blockheads as ever, only more proud and self-conceited.

If a man empties his purse into his head, no man can take it away from him. An investment in knowledge always pays the best interest.

The idea of what is true merit . . . as consisting in an inclination joined with an ability to serve mankind, one's country, friends and family . . . should indeed be the great aim and end of all learning.

Learning, whether speculative or practical, is in popular or mixed governments, the natural source of wealth and honor.

Genius is nothing but a greater aptitude for patience.

> *Some men grow mad by studying much to know,*
> *But who grows mad by studying good to grow.*

He that can compose himself is wiser than he that composes books.

A learned blockhead is a greater blockhead than an ignorant one.

Write with the learned, pronounce with the vulgar.

Let thy child's first lesson be obedience, and the second will be what thou wilt.

[Proposing an educational plan for the colony of Pennsylvania] Though the American youth are allowed not to want capacity, the best capacities require cultivation, it being truly with them, as with the best ground which, unless well tilled and sowed with profitable seed, produces only ranker weeds.

The doors of wisdom are never shut.

On Faith, Religion, & Enlightenment

In the affairs of this world men are saved, not by faith, but by the want of it.

Many have quarreled about religion that never practiced it.

Men differ daily about things which are subject to sense; is it likely then they should agree about things invisible?

Different sects like different clocks may be all near the matter though they don't quite agree.

Sam's religion is like a cheddar cheese, 'tis made of the milk of one and twenty parishes.

Sound, and sound doctrine, may pass through a ram's horn and a preacher, without straitening the one or amending the other.

Some make conscience of wearing a hat in the church who make none of robbing the altar.

How many observe Christ's birthday! How few, his precepts! O! 'tis easier to keep holidays than commandments.

> *That ignorance makes devout, if right the notion,*
> *'Troth, Rufus, thou'rt a man of great devotion.*

The faith you mention has doubtless its use in the world. I do not desire to see it diminished, nor would

I endeavor to lessen it in any man. But I wish it were more productive of good works than I have generally seen it; I mean real good works, works of kindness, charity, mercy, and public spirit; not holiday-keeping, sermon-reading, or hearing, performing church ceremonies, or making long prayers, filled with flatteries and compliments, despised even by wise men, and much less capable of pleasing the Deity.

Serving God is doing good to man, but praying is thought an easier service, and therefore more generally chosen.

A good example is the best sermon.

The worship of God is a duty; the hearing and reading of sermons may be useful; but, if men rest in hearing and praying, as too many do, it is as if a tree should value itself on being watered and putting forth leaves, though it never produced any fruit.

I do not think that thanks and compliments, though repeated weekly, can discharge our real obligations to each other, and much less those to our Creator.

When I stretch my imagination through and beyond our system of planets, beyond the visible fixed stars themselves into that space that is every way infinite, and conceive it filled with suns like ours, each with a chorus of worlds forever moving round him, then this little ball on which we move seems, even in my narrow imagination, to be almost nothing, and myself less than nothing and of no sort of consequence. When I think thus . . . I cannot conceive otherwise than that the Infinite Father expects or requires no worship or praise from us, but that he is infinitely above it.

But, since there is in all men something like a natural principle, which inclines them to *devotion,* or the worship of some unseen power;

And since men are endued with reason superior to all other animals, that we are in our world acquainted with;

Therefore I think it seems required of me, and my duty as a man, to pay divine regards to *something*.

The way to see by faith is to shut the eye of reason: The morning daylight appears plainer when you put out your candle.

To lead a virtuous life, my friends, and get to
Heaven in season,
You've just so much more need of faith, as
you have less of reason.

You men of reason and virtue are always dealing in mysteries, though you laugh at them when the church makes them.

You decline the trial of what is good by reason: And had rather make a bold attack upon Providence; the usual way of you gentlemen of fashion, who, when by living in defiance of the eternal rules of reason, you have plunged yourselves into a thousand difficulties, endeavor to make yourselves easy by throwing the burden upon nature.

On Fame

There have been as great souls unknown to fame as any of the most famous.

Bucephalus, the horse of Alexander hath as lasting fame as his master.

If you would not be forgotten, as soon as you are dead and rotten, either write things worth reading, or do things worth the reading.

Caesar did not merit the triumphal car more than he that conquers himself.

When out of favor, none know thee; when in, thou dost not know thyself.

Applause waits on success.

The *Tatler* tells of a girl who was observed to grow suddenly proud, and none could guess the reason till it came to be known that she had got on a pair of new silk garters. . . . I fear I have not so much reason to be proud as the girl had; for a feather in the cap is not so useful a thing, or so serviceable to the wearer, as a pair of good silk garters.

Admiration is the daughter of ignorance.

An ill wound, but not an ill name, may be healed.

A lean award is better than a fat judgment.

On Food & Appetite

Eat not to dullness; drink not to elevation.

A fat kitchen, a lean will.

The excellence of hogs is—fatness; of men—virtue.

Eat to live, and not live to eat.

If it were not for the belly, the back might wear gold.

Fools make feasts and wise men eat 'em.

To lengthen thy life, lessen thy meals.

Nine men in ten are suicides.

Too much plenty makes mouth dainty.

> *Cheese and salt meat, should be sparingly eat.*
> *Onions can make even heirs and widows weep.*

He that lives carnally, won't live eternally.

On Fools & Follies

Who knows a fool must know his brother;
For one will recommend another.

Wise men learn by others harms; Fools by their own.

The first degree of folly is to conceit oneself wise; the second to profess it; the third to despise counsel.

Fools need advice most, but wise men only are the better for it.

Fools multiply folly.

The fool hath made a vow, I guess,
Never to let the fire have peace.

As charms are nonsense, nonsense is a charm.

He's a fool that cannot conceal his wisdom.

On Friends & Foes

Life's a wilderness without a friend, and all its gilded scenes but barren and tasteless.

A brother may not be a friend, but a friend will always be a brother.

The same man cannot be both friend and flatterer.

Love your neighbor; yet don't pull down your hedge.

Relation without friendship, friendship without power, power without will, will without effect, effect without profit, and profit without virtue, are not worth a farto.

Friendship cannot live with ceremony, nor without civility.

Friends are the true sceptres of princes.

Be slow in choosing a friend, slower in changing.

You mention that you feel yourself hurt. Permit me to offer you a maxim, which has through life been of use to me. . . . It is, always to suppose one's friends may be right till one finds them wrong; rather than to suppose them wrong till one finds them right. You have heard and imagined all that can be said or supposed on one side of the question, but not on the other.

To be intimate with a foolish friend is like going to bed to a razor.

A false friend and a shadow attend only while the sun shines.

If you would keep your secret from an enemy tell it not to a friend.

Thou canst not joke an enemy into a friend, but thou mayest a friend into an enemy.

'Tis great confidence in a friend to tell him your faults, greater to tell him his.

Friendship increases by visiting friends, but by visiting seldom.

Love considered merely as a passion, will naturally have but a short duration; like all other passions 'tis changeable, transient and accidental. But friendship and esteem are derived from principles of reason and thought, and when once truly fixed in the mind, are lasting securities of an attachment to our persons and fortunes;

participate with, and refine all our joys; sympathize with, and blunt the edge of every adverse occurrence.

Wouldst thou confound thine enemy, be good thy self.

Do good to thy friend to keep him, to they enemy to gain him.

The wise man draws more advantage from his enemies, than the fool from his friends.

If you would be revenged of your enemy, govern your self.

Beware of meat twice boiled, and an old foe reconciled.

Some worth it argues, a friend's worth to know;
Virtue to own the Virtue of a Foe.

There is no little enemy.

You and I were long friend; you are now my enemy, and I am
Yours,
B. Franklin

On George Washington

George Washington, Commander of the American armies, who, like Joshua of old, commanded the sun and the moon to stand still, and they obeyed him.

Here you will know and enjoy what posterity will say of Washington. For a thousand leagues have nearly the same effect with a thousand years.

[From Franklin's Last Will and Testament] My fine crab-tree walking stick, with a gold head curiously wrought in the form of the cap of liberty, I give to my friend, and the friend of mankind, General Washington. If it were a scepter, he has merited it, and would become it.

On Gifts & Ingratitude

Constant complaint is the poorest sort of pay for all the comforts we enjoy.

Gifts much expected, are paid, not given.

He that has done you a kindness will be more ready to do you another, than he whom you yourself have obliged.

Most people return small favors, acknowledge middling ones, and repay great ones with ingratitude.

Blessed is he that expects nothing, for he shall never be disappointed.

On Houseguests

Fish and visitors smell in three days.

> *Visits should be short, like a winter's day,*
> *Lest you're too troublesome hasten away.*

> *If you would have guests merry with your cheer,*
> *Be so yourself, or so at least appear.*

If you'd lose a troublesome visitor, lend him money.

The busy man has few idle visitors; to the boiling pot the flies come not.

On How to Succeed in Life

The secret of success is constancy to purpose.

Thirteen virtues necessary for true success: temperance, silence, order, resolution, frugality, industry, sincerity, justice, moderation, cleanliness, tranquility, chastity and humility.

He that builds before he counts the cost, acts foolishly; and he that counts before he builds, finds he did not count wisely.

Patience in market, is worth pounds in a year.

An egg today is better than a hen tomorrow.

Cut the wings of your hens and hopes, lest they lead you a weary dance after them.

He that can have patience can have what he will.

Do not anticipate trouble, or worry about what may never happen. Keep in the sunlight.

Molehills, if often heaped, to mountains rise:
Weigh every small expence, and nothing waste,
Farthings long saved, amount to pounds at last.

Energy and persistence conquer all things.

Hold your council before dinner; the full belly hates thinking as well as acting.

The eye of the master will do more work than both his hands.

He who pursues two hares at once does not catch the one and lets the other go.

In success be moderate.

Great estates may venture more;
Little boats must keep near shore.

'Tis easier to build two chimneys, than maintain one in fuel.

Opportunity is the great bawd.

To be thrown upon one's own resources is to be cast into the very lap of fortune, for our faculties then undergo a development and display an energy of which they were previously unsusceptible.

Fortune is as fickle as she's fair.

Neither trust, nor contend, nor lay wagers, nor lend;
And you'll have peace to your lives end.

He that by the plow would thrive
Himself must either hold or drive.

God helps them that helps themselves.

Mine is better than ours.

Resolve to perform what you ought; perform without fail what you resolve.

He that can take rest is greater than he that can take cities.

There is neither honour nor gain, got in dealing with a villain.

———

Anoint a villain and he'll stab you, stab him and he'll anoint you.

Great famine when wolves eat wolves.

He that leith down with dogs, shall rise up with fleas.

He that would be beforehand in the world, must be beforehand with his business: It is not only ill management, but discovers a slothful disposition, to do that in the afternoon, which should have been done in the morning.

Discontented minds, and fevers of the body, are not to be cured by changing beds or businesses.

Useful attainments in your minority will procure riches in maturity, of which writing and accounts are not the meanest.

Nothing humbler than ambition, when it is about to climb.

Hope of gain
Lessens pain.

———

'Tis a laudable ambition, that aims at being better than his neighbours.

Ambition has its disappointments to sour us, but never the good fortune to satisfy us.

Strive to be the greatest man in your country, and you may be disappointed. Strive to be the best and you may succeed: he may well win the race that runs by himself.

On Human Error

None but the well-bred man knows how to confess a fault, or acknowledge himself in an error.

The wise and the brave dares own that he was wrong.

The sting of a reproach is the truth of it.

To err is human, to repent divine; to persist devilish.

The brave and the wise can both pity and excuse; when cowards and fools shew no Mercy.

What pains our Justice takes his faults to hide,
With half that pains sure he might cure 'em quite.

He that can bear a reproof, and mend by it, if he is not wise, is in a fair way of being so.

On Industry & Merit

Industry need not wish.

Fatigue is the best pillow.

No man e'er was glorious, who was not laborious.

Without industry and frugality, nothing will do, and with them everything.

Sloth, like rust, consumes faster than labor wears; the used key is always bright.

Jack Little sowed little, and little he'll reap.

He that hath a trade hath an estate; and he that hath a calling, hath an office of profit and honour.

———

Early to bed and early to rise make a man healthy, wealthy and wise.

Diligence is the mother of good luck.

Little Strokes,
Fell great Oaks.

Work as if you were to live a hundred years, pray as if you were to die tomorrow.

He that lives upon hope will die fasting.

He that waits upon fortune is never sure of a dinner.

Be not sick too late, nor well too soon.

He that riseth late must trot all day, and shall scarce overtake his business at night.

Laziness travels so slowly that Poverty soon overtakes him.

All things are easy to industry,
All things difficult to sloth.

———

A little neglect may breed great mischief . . . for want of a nail the shoe was lost; for want of a shoe the horse was lost; and for want of a horse the rider was lost.

Perform, and with thy prudence guide thy fate.

At the workingman's house hunger looks in, but dares not enter.

Industry pays debts, while despair increases them.

> *Plow deep while sluggards sleep,*
> *and you shall have corn to sell and to keep.*

There are lazy minds as well as lazy bodies.

Cunning proceeds from want of capacity.

Be neither silly, nor cunning, but wise.

You may be too cunning for one, but not for all.

Many would live by their wits, but break for want of stock.

When men are employed, they are best contented; for on the days they worked they were good-natured and cheerful, and, with the consciousness of having done a good day's work, they spent the evening jollily; but on our idle days they were mutinous and quarrelsome.

On Justice & the Courts

That it is better one hundred guilty persons should escape than that one innocent person should suffer is a maxim that has been long and generally approved.

Without justice, courage is weak.

Innocence is its own defense.

Suspicion may be no fault, but shewing it may be a great one.

> *To friend, lawyer, doctor, tell plain your whole case;*
> *Nor think on bad matters to put a good face:*
> *How can they advise, if they see but a part?*
> *'Tis very ill driving black hogs in the dark.*

Pardoning the bad is injuring the good.

On Lawyers

A countryman between two lawyers is like a fish between two cats.

Lawyers, preachers, and tomtits eggs, there are more of them hatched than come to perfection.

Necessity has no law; I know some attorneys of the name.

> *God works wonders now and then;*
> *Behold! a lawyer, an honest man!*

On Liberty

Those who live under arbitrary power do nevertheless aprove of liberty, and wish for it; they almost despair of recovering it in Europe; they read the translations of our separate colony constitutions with rapture; and there are such numbers everywhere, who talk of removing to America . . . it is generally believed we shall have a prodigious addition of strength, wealth and arts from the emigration of Europe; and it is thought that to lessen or prevent such emigrations, the tyrannies established there must relax, and allow more liberty to their people. Hence it is a common observation here that our cause is the cause of all mankind, and that we are fighting for their liberty in defending our own.

Where liberty dwells, there is my country.—*Attributed*

God grant that not only the love of liberty but a thorough knowledge of the rights of man may pervade all the nations of the earth, so that a philosopher may set his foot anywhere on its surface and say: "This is my country."

They that can give up essential liberty to obtain a little temporary safety deserve neither liberty nor safety.

Nothing brings more pain than too much pleasure; nothing more bondage than too much liberty.

Everything one has a right to do is not best to be done.

Without freedom of thought there can be no such thing as wisdom; and no such thing as liberty without freedom of speech.

Sudden power is apt to be insolent, sudden liberty saucy; that behaves best which has grown gradually.

[From a comic epitaph to his daughter Deborah's pet squirrel]

Learn hence,
Ye who blindly seek more liberty,
Whether subjects, sons, squirrels or daughters,
That apparent restraint may be real protection;
Yielding peace and plenty
With security.

ON LOVE & MARRIAGE

He that takes a wife takes care.

A single man . . . is an incomplete animal. He resembles the odd half of a pair of scissors.

Happy's the owing, that's not long a doing.

Where there's marriage without love, there will be love without marriage.

You cannot pluck roses without fear of thorns,
Nor enjoy a fair wife without danger of horns.

Love, cough and a smoke can't well be hid.

Keep your eyes wide open before marriage, half shut afterwards.

A ship under sail and a big-bellied woman are the handsomest two things that can be seen as common.

Why does a blind man's wife paint herself?

There are no ugly loves, nor handsome prisons.

If you would be loved, love and be lovable.

Marry your son when you will, but your daughter when you can.

A house without woman and firelight,
Is like a body without soul or sprite.

The proof of gold is fire, the proof of woman, gold; the proof of man, a woman.

Grief for a dead wife, and a troublesome guest,
Continues to the threshold, and there is at rest;
But I mean such wives as are none of the best.

Ne'er take a wife till thou hast a house (and a fire) to put her in.

When a man and woman die, as poets sung,
His heart's the last part moves—her last, the tongue.

A good wife lost is God's gift lost.

Women are books, and the men the readers be,
Who sometimes in those books erratas see;
Yet oft the reader's raptured with each line,
Fair print and paper, fraught with sense divine;
Though some, neglectful, seldom care to read,
And faithful wives no more than Bibles heed.
Are woman books? says Hodge, then would mine were
An almanac, to change her every year.

Love and toothache have many cures, but none infallible except possession and dispossession.

Wedlock, as old men note, hath likened been,
Unto a public crowd or common rout;

Where those that are without would fain get in,
And those that are within, would fain get out.
Grief often treads upon the heels of pleasure,
Married in haste, we oft repent at leisure;
Some by experience find these words misplaced,
Married at leisure, they repent in haste.

＊

ON MONEY

The use of money is all the advantage there is in having money.

Nothing but money
Is sweeter than honey.

He that is of [the] opinion money will do everything, may well be suspected of doing everything for money.

There are three faithful friends—an old wife, an old dog, and ready money.

If you would know the value of money, go and try to borrow some.

May not luxury produce more than it consumes . . . ?
A shilling spent idly by a fool may be picked up by a
wiser person, who knows better what to do with it.

Almost all the parts of our bodies require some expense.
The feet demand shoes; the legs, stockings; the rest of
the body, clothing; and the belly, a good deal of victuals.
Our eyes, though exceedingly useful, ask, when reasonable, only the cheap assistance of spectacles. . . . But
the eyes of other people are the eyes that ruin us. If all
but myself were blind, I should want neither fine
clothes, fine houses, nor fine furniture.

On Opinions

We are men, all subject to errors. Our opinions are not
in our own power; they are formed and governed much
by circumstances that are often as inexplicable as they
are irresistible.

Since it is no more in a man's power to think than to
look like another, methinks all that should be expected
from me is to keep my mind open to conviction, to
hear patiently and attentively, whatever is offered me for

that end; and, if after all I continue in the same errors, I believe your usual charity will induce you to rather pity and excuse than blame me.

I think opinions should be judged of by their influences and effects; and, if a man holds none that tend to make his less virtuous or more vicious, it may be concluded he holds none that are dangerous; which I hope is the case with me.

Singularity in the right, hath ruined many: Happy those who are convinced of the general opinion.

The horse thinks one thing, and he that saddles him another.

On Passions & Pleasures

The end of passion is the beginning of repentance.

He is a governor that governs his passions, and he a servant that serves them.

Our necessities never equal our wants.

Great good-nature, without prudence, is a great misfortune.

Keep conscience clear,
Then never fear.

A man in a passion rides a mad horse.

'Tis easier to suppress the first desire than to satisfy all that follow it.

Sin is not hurtful because it is forbidden, but it is forbidden because it is hurtful.

Many a man thinks he is buying pleasure, when he is really selling himself a slave to it.

What maintains one vice would bring up two children.

Pain wastes the body; pleasures, the understanding.

Would you live with ease,
Do what you ought,
And not what you please.

Where sense is wanting, everything is wanting.

If man could have half his wishes, he would double his troubles.

On a Penny Saved

A penny saved is two pence clear,
A pin a day's a groat a year.

All things are cheap to the saving, dear to the wasteful.

Light purse, heavy heart.

Ere you consult your fancy, consult your purse.

Gain may be temporary and uncertain, but ever while you live, expense is constant and certain.

Beware of little expenses; a small leak will sink a great ship.

The thrifty maxim of the wary Dutch,
Is to save all the money they can touch.

He that is rich need not live sparingly, and he that can live sparingly need not be rich.

A man has no more goods than he gets good by.

Spare and have is better than spend and crave.

In short, I conceive that a great part of the miseries of mankind are brought upon them by the false estimates they have made of the value of things, and by their giving too much for their whistles.

> *For age and want save while you may;*
> *No morning sun lasts a whole day.*

When prosperity was well mounted, she let go the bridle, and soon came tumbling out of the saddle.

On People in General

Men and melons are hard to know.

Mankind are very odd creatures. One half censure what they practice, the other half practice what they censure; the rest always say and do as they ought.

Men meet, mountains never.

In my own private concerns with mankind, I have observed that to kick a little when under imposition, has a good effect. A little sturdiness when superiors are much in the wrong, sometimes occasions consideration. And there is truth in the old saying, that if you make yourself a sheep, the wolves will eat you.

A mob's a monster; heads enough but no brains.

There are three things extremely hard: steel, a diamond and to know one's self.

Most fools think they are only ignorant.

Ignorance leads men into a party, and shame keeps them from getting out again.

It is common for men to give pretended reasons instead of one real one.

To bear other people's afflictions, everyone has courage and enough to spare.

Our reason would be of more use to *us*, if it would prevent *the* evils it can hardly enable us to *bear*. But in *that* it is so *deficient*, and in other things so often *misleads us*, *that* I have *sometimes* been almost tempted to wish we had *been furnished* with a good sensible instinct instead of it.

Who judges best of a man, his enemies or himself?

On the Art of Persuasion

If you have no honey in your *pot*, have some in your mouth.

Would you persuade, speak of interest, not of reason

He that would catch fish, must venture his bait.

Reasonable, sensible men can always make a reasonable scheme appear such to other reasonable men, if they take pains and have time and opportunity for it, unless from some circumstances their honesty and good intentions are suspected.

So convenient a thing it is to be a reasonable creature, since it enables one to find or make a reason for everything one has a mind to do.

When Reason preaches, if you won't hear her she'll box your ears.

Poor plain dealing! dead without issue!

I received your letter. . . . My vanity might possibly be flattered by your expressions of compliment to my understanding, if your proposals did not more clearly manifest a mean opinion of it.

He that would rise at court, must begin by creeping.

ON POVERTY & RICHES

The poor have little, beggars none, the rich too much, enough not one.

Where bread is wanting, all's to be sold.

Having been poor is no shame, but being ashamed of it is.

Poverty often deprives a man of all spirit and virtue; it is hard for an empty bag to stand upright.

Necessity never made a good bargain.

When the well's dry, we know the worth of water.

Hunger never saw bad bread.

'Tis hard (but glorious) to be poor and honest: An empty sack can hardly stand upright; but if it does, 'tis a stout one!

A little house well filled, a little field well tilled, and a little wife well willed, are great riches.

Wealth and Content are not always bedfellows.

He that hath no ill fortune will be troubled with good.

Content makes poor men rich; Discontent makes rich men poor.

He does not possess wealth that allows it to possess him.

Content is the philosopher's stone that turns all it touches into gold.

Better is a little with content than too much with contention.

He that's content, hath enough; He that complains has too much.

Human felicity is produced not so much by great pieces of good fortune that seldom happen, as by little advantages that occur every day.

On Pride & Self-Worth

Pride gets into the coach, and Shame mounts behind.

As sore places meet most rubs, proud folks meet most affronts.

Pride is as loud a beggar as want, and a great deal more saucy.

Pride breakfasted with Plenty, dined with Poverty, supped with Infamy.

Pride dines upon vanity, sups on contempt.

The proud hate pride—in others.

He that falls in love with himself will have no rivals.

A man wrapped up in himself makes a very small bundle.

Pride is said to be the last vice the good man gets clear of. 'Tis a mere Proteus, and disguises itself under all manner of appearances, putting on sometimes even the mask of humility. If some are proud of neatness and propriety of dress; others are equally so of despising it, and acting the perpetual sloven.

Declaiming against pride is not always a sign of humility.

Great merit is coy, as well as great pride.

Most people dislike vanity in others, whatever share they have of it themselves; but I give it fair quarter wherever I meet with it, being persuaded that it is often productive of good to the possessor, and to others that are within his sphere of action; and therefore, in many cases, it would not be altogether absurd if a man were to thank God for his vanity among the other comforts of life.

Great modesty often hides great merit.

Tho' modesty is a virtue, bashfulness is a vice.

Hide not your talents, they for use were made.
What's a sun-dial in the Shade!

A cipher and humility make the other figures and virtues of tenfold value.

To be humble to superiors is duty, to equals courtesy, to inferiors nobleness.

Scandal, like other virtues, is in part its own reward, as it gives us the satisfaction of making ourselves appear better than others, or others no better than ourselves.

On Principles of
Government

The magistrate should obey the laws, the people should obey the magistrate.

He that cannot obey, cannot command.

Much of the strength and efficiency of any government, in procuring and securing happiness to the people, depends on opinion, on the general opinion that the goodness of that government, as well as of the wisdom and integrity of its governors.

In rivers and bad governments, the lightest things swim at top.

The good will of the governed will be starved, if not fed by the good deeds of the governors.

The longer I live, the more convincing proofs I see of this truth, that God governs in the affairs of men. And if a sparrow cannot fall to the ground without his notice, is it probable that an empire can rise without his aid?

It has been computed by some political arithmetician that, if every man and woman would work for four hours each day on something useful, labor would produce sufficient to procure all the necessaries and comforts of life, want and misery would be banished out of the world, and the rest of the 24 hours might be leisure and pleasure.

A virtuous and laborious people may be cheaply governed.

There is no kind of dishonesty into which otherwise good people more easily and more frequently fall than that of defrauding the government.

Laws like to cobwebs catch small flies,
Great ones break thro' before your eyes.

Laws too gentle are seldom obeyed; too severe, seldom executed.

Where carcasses are, eagles will gather,
And where good laws are, much people flock thither.

On Public Office

I shall never ask, never refuse, nor ever resign an office.

To serve the public faithfully, and at the same time please it entirely, is impracticable.

The first mistake in public business is the going into it.

You may give a man an office, but you cannot give him discretion.

When I am employed in serving others, I do not look upon myself as conferring favors, but as paying debts. . . . I have received much kindness from men, to whom I shall never have any opportunity of making the least direct return, and numberless mercies from God, who is infinitely above being benefited by our services.

One would think that a man so laboring disinterestedly for the good of his fellow creatures could not possibly by such means make himself enemies; but there are minds who cannot bear that another should distinguish himself even by greater usefulness; and though he demands no profit, nor anything in return but the good will of those he is serving, they will endeavor to deprive him of that, first by disputing the truth of his experiments, then their utility; and, being defeated there, they finally dispute his right to them, and would give the credit of them to a man that lived 3000 years ago, or at 3000 leagues distance, rather than to a neighbor or even a friend.

I think the offense much greater in those who, either directly or indirectly, have been concerned in making the very laws they break. . . . I cannot help thinking there are still those in the world who can see a mote in their brother's eye, while they do not discern a beam in their own and that the old saying is as true now as ever it was, "One man may better steal a horse than another look over the hedge."

What must we think of sen[ato]rs who can evade paying for their wheels [tax on carriage wheels] or their plate, in defiance of law and justice, and yet declaim against corruption, as if their own hearts and hands were pure and unsullied?

It is wonderful how preposterously the affairs of this world are managed. Naturally one would imagine that the interest of a few individuals should give way to general interest; but individuals manage their affairs with so much more application, industry and address, than the public do theirs, that general interest most commonly gives way to particular.

Whatever some may think and say, it is worthwhile to do men good, for the self-satisfaction one has in the reflection.

On Scientific Experiment

Man: A tool-making animal.

What signifies knowing the names, if you know not the natures of things.

Furnished as all Europe now is with academies of science, with nice instruments and the spirit of experiment, the progress of human knowledge will be rapid, and discoveries made of which we have at present no conception. I begin to be almost sorry I was born so soon, since I cannot have the happiness of knowing what will be known 100 years hence.

———

[Asked about a new invention "what good is it?", Franklin replied] What good is a newborn baby?

It is of real use to know that china left in the air unsupported will fall and break; but how it comes to fall and why it breaks are matters of speculation. It is a pleasure indeed to know them, but we can preserve our china without it.

Chagrined a little that we have hitherto been able to produce nothing in this way of use to mankind, and the hot weather coming on, when electrical experiments are not so agreeable, it is proposed to put an end to them for this season, somewhat humorously, in a party of pleasure on the banks of the Schuylkill. Spirits, at the same time, are to be fired by a spark sent from side to side through the river, without any other conductor than the water. . . . A turkey is to be killed for our dinner by the electrical jack, before a fire kindled by the electrified bottle; when the healths of all the famous electricians in England, Holland, France and Germany are to be drunk in electrified bumpers, under the discharge of guns from the electrical battery.

[Simple observations and logic prompt an experiment to determine if electricity is present in lightning] Electrical fluid agrees with lightning in these particulars: 1. Giving light. 2. Color of the light. 3. Crooked direction. 4. Swift motion. 5. Being conducted by metals. 6. Crack or noise on exploding. 7. Subsiding in water or ice. 8. Rending bodies it passes through. 9. Destroying animals. 10. Molting metals. 11. Firing inflammable substances. 12. Sulfurous smell. . . . Since they agree in all particulars wherein we can already compare them, is it not probable that they agree likewise? Let the experiment be made.

[Hearing that George III ordered the blunt rods on top of Kew Palace be substituted for Franklin's pointed lightning rod, because an American type rod was not patriotic for an English palace] The King's changing his pointed conductors for blunt is a matter of small importance to me. If I had a wish about it, it would be that he rejected them altogether as ineffectual. For it is only since he thought himself and family safe from the thunder of Heaven, that he dared to use his own thunder in destroying his innocent subjects.

[Franklin published his inventions but refused to patent them] These thoughts are . . . crude and hasty; and if I were merely ambitious of acquiring some reputation in philosophy I ought to keep them by me till corrected and improved by time and further experience. But since even short hints and imperfect experiments in any new branch of science, being communicated, have oftimes a good effect in exciting the attention of the ingenious to the subject, and so become the occasion of more exact disquisition and more complete discoveries, you are at liberty to communicate this paper to whom you please; it being of more importance that knowledge should increase than that your friend should be thought an accurate philosopher.

On "Society"

All blood is alike ancient.

He is not well-bred, that cannot bear ill-breeding in others.

Savages we call them because their manners differ from ours.

Adam was never called Master Adam; we never read of Noah Esquire, Lot Knight and Baronet, nor the Right

Honorable Abraham, Viscount Mesopotamia, Baron of Carian; no, no, they were plain men.

Don't value a man for the quality he is of, but for the qualities he possesses.

An innocent plowman is more worthy than a vicious prince.

Glass, china and reputation are easily cracked, and never well mended.

Benignity of mind which shows itself in searching for and seizing every opportunity to serve and oblige; and is the foundation of what is called good breeding, highly useful to the possessor, and most agreeable to all.

Ceremony is not civility; nor civility ceremony.

'Tis a shame that your family is an honor to you! You ought to be an honor to your family.

On Time

What we call time enough always proves little enough.

Up, sluggard, and waste not life; in the grave will be sleeping enough.

Lost time is never found again.

Dost thou love life? Then do not squander time; for that's the stuff life is made of.

Remember that time is money.

There's a time to wink as well as to see.

Employ thy time well, if thou meanest to gain leisure.

A child thinks twenty shillings and twenty years can scarce ever be spent.

'Tis easy to see, hard to foresee.

Since thou art not sure of a minute, throw not away an hour.

You may delay, but time will not.

On Too Much Talk

A pair of good ears will drain dry a hundred tongues.

The wise understand half a word.

You may talk too much on the best of subjects.

Here comes the orator! with his flood of words, and his drop of reason.

Words may shew a man's wit, but actions his meaning.

Don't overload gratitude; if you do, she'll kick.

Great talkers should be cropped, for they have no need of ears.

Teach your child to hold his tongue, he'll learn fast enough to speak.

———

Better slip with foot than tongue.

Mary's mouth costs her nothing, for she never opens it but at others expense.

Man's tongue is soft, and bone doth lack;
Yet a stroke therewith may break a man's back.

When you speak to a man, look on his eyes; when he speaks to thee, look on his mouth.

The heart of a fool is in his mouth, but the mouth of a wise man is in his heart.

It is ill-manners to silence a fool, and cruelty to let him go on.

Tongue double, brings trouble.

Keep your mouth wet, feet dry.

Harry Smatter,
Has a Mouth for every Matter.

———

Half-wits talk much but say little.

The wit of conversation consists more in finding it in others than showing a great deal yourself.

Great talkers, little doers.

A word to the wise is enough, and many words won't fill a bushel.

A great talker may be no fool, but he is one that relies on him.

On the United States Constitution

The United States Constitution doesn't guarantee happiness, only the pursuit of it: You have to catch up with it yourself.

Our new Constitution is now established, and has an appearance that promises permanency; but in this world nothing can be said to be certain, except death and taxes.

The delegates generally appointed . . . are men of character . . . so that I hope good from their meeting. Indeed if it does not do good it must do harm, as it will show that we have not wisdom enough among us to govern ourselves and will strengthen the opinion of some political writers that popular governments cannot long support themselves.

[Franklin motions that sessions might be opened with prayer] In this situation of this assembly, groping, as it were, in the dark, to find political truth, and scarce able to distinguish it when presented to us, how is it happened, sir, that we have not hitherto once thought of humbly applying to the Father of Lights to illuminate our understandings?

I confess that I do not entirely approve of this Constitution at present; but, sir, I am not sure I shall never approve it; for having lived long, I have experienced many instances of being obliged, by better information or fuller consideration, to change opinions even on important subjects, which I once through right, but found to be otherwise.

When you assemble a number of men, to have the advantage of their joint wisdom, you inevitably assemble with those men all their prejudices, their passions, their errors of opinion, their local interests, and their selfish views. Form such an assembly can a perfect production be expected?

I consent, sir, to this Constitution, because I expect no better, and because I am not sure that it is not the best. The opinions I have had of its errors I sacrifice to the public good.

Sir, I cannot help expressing a wish that every member of the convention who may still have objections to [the Constitution] would with me on this occasion doubt a little of his own infallibility, and, to make manifest our unanimity, put his name to this instrument.

On Virtue, the Good Life, & a Good Example

The noblest question in the world is, "What good may I do in it?"

There is no man so bad but he secretly respects the good.

He is ill clothed, who is bare of virtue.

Beatus esse sine virtute, nemo potest.

What is more valuable than gold? Diamonds. Than diamonds? Virtue.

Sell not virtue to purchase wealth, nor liberty to purchase power.

Hast thou virtue?—acquire also the graces and beauties of virtue.

Each year, one vicious habit rooted out, in time ought to make the worst man good.

A good man is seldom uneasy, an ill one never easy.

A wicked hero will turn his back to an innocent coward.

When you're good to others, you are best to yourself.

The rotten apple spoils his companion.

Setting too good an example is a kind of slander seldom forgiven; 'tis *Scandalum Magnatum*.

Well done is better than well said.

None preaches better than the ant, and she says nothing.

There is much difference between imitating a good man and counterfeiting him.

Observe all men; thyself most.

A long life may not be good enough, but a good life is long enough.

On War, Peace, and Our Readiness for Both

War brings scars.

There never was a good war or a bad peace.

We made daily improvements in *natural*, there is one I wish to see in *moral* philosophy; the discovery of a plan that would induce and oblige nations to settle their disputes without first cutting one another's throats.

I have never yet known of a peace made that did not occasion a great deal of popular discontent, clamor, and censure on both sides. This is, perhaps, owing to the usual management of the ministers and leaders of the contending nations, who to keep up the spirits of their people for continuing the war, generally represent the state of their own affairs in a better light, and that of the enemy in a worse, than is consistent with the truth; hence the populace on each side expect better terms than really can be obtained, and are apt to ascribe their disappointment to treachery. So that the blessing promised to peacemakers, I fancy relates to the next world, for in this they seem to have a greater chance of being cursed.

When will men be convinced that even successful wars at length become misfortunes to those who unjustly commenced them, and who triumphed blindly in their success, not seeing all its consequences? Your great comfort and mine in this war is that we honestly and faithfully did everything in our power to prevent it.

Courage would fight, but discretion won't let him.

[Urging America to keep a standing army] The expenses required to prevent a war are much lighter than those that will, if not prevented, be absolutely necessary to maintain it.

He that's secure is not safe.

Distrust and caution are the parents of security.

Forewarned, forearmed.—Proverb recycled by Franklin from Miguel Cervantes's *Don Quixote, 1615.*

They that are on their guard and appear ready to receive their adversaries, are in much less danger of being attacked than the supine, secure and negligent.

A few years of peace will improve, will restore and increase, our strength; but our future safety will depend on our union and virtue. . . . Let us beware of being lulled into a dangerous security; and of being both en-

ervated and impoverished by luxury; of being weak-
ened by internal contentions and divisions; of being
shamefully extravagant in contracting private debts,
while we are backward in discharging honorable those
of the public.

BENJAMIN FRANKLIN
(1 7 0 6 — 1 7 9 0)

Benjamin Franklin, one of America's founding fathers and foremost men of letters, is forever associated with the red-bricked streets and buildings of eighteenth-century Philadelphia, but Boston was his birthplace and early home. He lived and apprenticed there until setting out on his own at age seventeen. His father was a candle and soap maker who kept a pious, Puritan household. His mother was his father's second wife, so while Benjamin was the eighth of ten children he was also the tenth son of his father's seventeen children. No wonder young Benjamin grew to be so frugal and self-reliant. Franklin abandoned his family's religion, but he held firmly to its puritanical ethos of serious purpose in life—a lesson that was also good for business. The industrious and thrifty young Franklin rose from rags to riches as a printer and author, retiring at the early age of forty-two to devote himself to his two consuming passions, science and government.

Though precocious in youth, Franklin had little formal education. At age twelve he was indentured to his brother James, nine years his senior and the printer and publisher of a free-thinking, often opinionated, sometimes radical newspaper called *The New England Courant.* During the five years Benjamin worked for James, from 1718 to 1723, he mastered the printer's trade. He read voraciously and, through his brother's influence, became conversant in modern Enlightenment thought. All the while James continued to print what Boston's other two papers would not, including a fictitious letter that discredited the Boston establishment and landed him in prison for libel. James served only a short sentence, but was prohibited upon release to either print or publish his paper. He skirted that order by discharging Ben from his apprenticeship two years early and naming him the paper's publisher of record. A new contract was drawn up in secret to keep Ben indentured those remaining two years, but the younger Franklin could no longer think of himself as his brother's apprentice.

Perhaps Benjamin felt slighted after having taken on additional responsibilities at the paper during his brother's confinement. Maybe he could no longer tolerate the physical blows and humiliation that were often a part of the master-apprentice relationship. Or, just maybe, as Franklin later wrote in his *Autobiography,* "perhaps I was too saucy and provoking." It was hard for the young Franklin not to be cocky since, by age fifteen, he was already accustomed to seeing his own writings in print beside that of the town's leading illuminati.

Franklin wrote for the *Courant* under the pen name Silence Dogwood, a fictitious and meddlesome widow concerned with issues relating to women, religion, free speech, the dangers of drink, and the vanities of fashionable dress. This widow also had an unusually resentful attitude toward Harvard University and those young men who, unlike Franklin, could afford to attend it. There were fourteen "Dogwood" papers in all. Printed anonymously at first, their authorship became known and brought the teenage Franklin much praise.

The brothers quarreled. Two months after James's release, their differences were irreconcilable. Benjamin rebelled by asserting his freedom, knowing that his brother could not go to the law and admit his defiance of the court order. James retaliated by blackballing him with printers in Boston and, later, New York. About his actions Franklin later wrote, "It was not fair in me to take this advantage and this I therefore reckon one of the first errata of my life."

After failing to find work in New York, Franklin ventured to Philadelphia where his fortune changed almost immediately. Within weeks of his arrival he was employed as a printer. By 1724 he found himself a patron in Sir William Keith, the governor of Pennsylvania. Keith was impressed with the ambitious young man and encouraged Franklin to open a shop of his own. But a trip to Boston for the purpose of seeking investors ended in failure when his father refused to support him saying he was too young to be in business for himself.

Governor Keith disagreed and offered to become Franklin's investor. He sent Ben to England to continue his education as a printer. London, vibrant and exciting, was a far cry from Puritan Boston and by all reports Franklin made the most of it, spending his time with "interesting" women and aspiring writers. Along the way he honed his skills as a master printer and made connections with stationers and booksellers that would eventually serve him well. He did this, by the way, without the aid of Governor Keith who turned out to be a man of debts and ill repute in his home country. The trust Franklin had put in Keith, setting sail for England with only his promise of patronage, paints a portrait of a young man either naive or blinded by ambition, or a little of both. The fact that he was not long disillusioned says something about his overriding pragmatism and his ever ready adaptability.

Much about Franklin changed during his stay in London, but not his capacity for hard work. In 1726 he returned home to Philadelphia to launch a thriving printing business. He also opened a bookshop, published the *Pennsylvania Gazette,* and in 1732 he introduced, under the pseudonym of Richard Stroud, *Poor Richard's Almanack.* The yearly almanacs popularized the serious lessons of a conduct book by interspersing them with witty, entertaining adages and aphorisms on life, marriage, the weather, and good business practice. While the character behind all this moralizing may have been fictitious (and profit-driven), Franklin truly believed that hard work, thrift, and honesty were all a man needed to succeed and find happiness. *Poor Richard* was an instant success and was condensed into an oft-reprinted international best-seller called *The Way to Wealth.*

In 1730 Franklin married Deborah Read. The couple had been engaged before Franklin left for London but, as time passed and Ben philandered, she married another man. By the time Franklin returned, Deborah had suffered the disgrace of learning that her husband had another wife in England as well as insurmountable debts on both sides of the Atlantic. He had skipped town for the West Indies and was rumored dead, leaving Deborah neither single, nor married nor widow. So why did the ambitious and socially minded Franklin choose Deborah? We know that he was not without disgrace himself, having begat an illegitimate child, William, whom Deborah accepted and raised as her own.

The couple married by common law, living together before announcing their union publicly. Deborah gave birth to a daughter, Sally, with whom Franklin would often correspond during his long stays abroad. Franklin was very close to his son, William, whom he only later regarded as bastard. William, a prominent loyalist and the governor of New Jersey, had a much publicized rift with his father over politics and the American Revolution.

Franklin began his political career early in Philadelphia, decades before the Revolution. In 1727, only one year after establishing shop in that city, he organized a group of intellectually fashionable young merchants into an active social force. They called themselves the "Junto," and by 1747 they had established a circulating library, a fire company, the American Philosophical Society, a college that would become the University of Pennsylvania, an insurance company, a city hospital, and a fully equipped voluntary militia. Involvement in public affairs soon brought Franklin appointments. He served as deputy postmaster for Philadelphia and as clerk of the General Assembly of Pennsylvania.

The American Philosophical Society deserves special mention. Philosophy, during the mid-eighteenth century, meant science. When Franklin retired in 1748, he fully intended to spend the rest of his days making scientific experiments. This goal was not inconsistent with his role in public affairs, since at the heart of both pursuits was his firm and enlightened belief in the capacity of men to understand themselves and affect the world at large.

As a scientist and inventor, Franklin explored theoretical matters to practical ends. He devised the Franklin Stove, a cast-iron inset that burned less wood and gave off more heat than open fireplaces. He proved that lightning was indeed a form of electricity with his famous kite and key experiment, and invented a lightning rod that to this day protects rooftops across the world. He formulated theories of heat absorption, measurement of the Gulf Stream (likening it to a river within the ocean), and techniques for tracking storm paths. In his spare time he invented bifocal lenses. Franklin published the results of his experiments but refused to patent his inventions. His contributions to science, like government, were a public service for which he thought compensation imprudent. True public service could only be magnanimous, without expectation of profit, as Franklin later advised in a motion to suppress salaries at the Philadelphia Convention in 1787,

> Ambition and avarice . . . Separately, each of these has great force in prompting men to action; but when united in view of the same object, they have in many minds the most violent effects. . . . Of what kind are the men that will strive for this profitable pre-eminence through all the bustle of cabal, the heat of contention, the infinite mutual abuse of parties, tearing to pieces the best of characters? It will not be the wise and moderate, the lovers of peace and good order, the men fittest for trust.

Public congratulations was, however, something Franklin never challenged; he proudly accepted membership into England's elite Royal Society in 1756, and the French Academy of Science in 1772.

Franklin's work in public affairs found him addressing Colonial grievances with England, culminating in the War for Independence. He served as member of the Philadelphia Council, Commissioner of the Peace, representative in the Pennsylvania Assembly, deputy postmaster general of North America, and chairman of Pennsylvania's Committee of Safety. His greatest contribution and longest post occurred, however, in Europe rather than America. He served as Colonial agent, a type of lobbyist, for several American colonies in England between 1757 and 1775. In London he weathered a succession of crises, the most legendary of these being the Stamp Act. Franklin never came out in favor of this act, but after Parliament passed it he dutifully ordered stamps for himself and nominated a friend for the post of stamp officer in Philadelphia. Perhaps the ocean had caused a schism between Franklin and his American brethren, for he greatly underestimated the intensity of their feelings on this matter. Deborah, fearful of their house being robbed, called upon male relatives for armed defense. Hearing of this clamor in London, Franklin did an about-face and appeared before the House of Commons. His was a dramatic defense, answering a total of 174 questions before the somewhat hostile assembly with dignity, logic, and eloquence. The Stamp Act was repealed shortly thereafter.

When the war broke, Franklin was a seventy-year-old revolutionary. He had left London aware that there might be bloodshed. Before his departure, he was called before the House of Commons once again. Like a rebellious child, they publicly scolded him for his role in the publication of the Hutchinson-Oliver letters, a once-private exchange between the governor of Massachusetts and his British superiors urging a stronger military presence in that colony. Franklin grieved much over his humiliation before Parliament and his ensuing fall from the social graces of London. The ultimate spin doctor, Franklin used the wrath he suffered in England to make himself a hero at home and, later, France.

The day after his arrival in Philadelphia, Franklin was made a delegate to the Second Continental Congress. He attended sessions from 1775 to 1776 and served on the commission that drafted the Declaration of Independence. In 1776, shortly after attending the constitutional convention for Pennsylvania, Franklin was appointed American diplomat to France. He lived in Paris until 1785 wheedling money and arms out of the French, attending to complaints by merchants and ship captains of Congress's relentless overspending, and all the while wooing the French crown into a crucial alliance with America. In his fur cap, spectacles, and plain brown clothes, Franklin promoted an image of America as a frontierland of humble, uncorrupted nobility and became quite the rage of Paris. His portrait was everywhere, on objets d'art from snuffboxes to chamber pots. His society was sought after by diplomats, scientists, Freemasons, and, most especially, the fashionable ladies.

Franklin stayed on in Europe to negotiate a peace settlement with Britain, then returned home to Philadelphia. Deborah had died during his absence, never setting eyes on her husband for the last ten years of her life. Franklin lived with his daughter Sally, her husband, and her small child. In 1785, nearing his eightieth birthday, he began a four-year term as president (governor) of Pennsylvania. In 1787 he assumed the presidency of the nation's first abolitionist society, a group founded by the Quakers with the title "The Pennsylvania Society for Promoting the Abolition of Slavery, and the Relief of Free Negroes Unlawfully Held In Bondage." He campaigned extensively to abolish slavery and even stated in his last will and testament that a family member would not receive their bequest if they did not first set free their negro slave.

Franklin's last appearance on the national scene was as a delegate to the Philadelphia Convention, which framed the United States Constitution in 1787. The drafting of that document was in the hands of delegates a great deal younger than Franklin, but it was his voice of reason that urged on an often stalled convention. During that long summer, he was a forceful advocate for the signing and ratification of a document with which he did not fully agree, but strongly believed was the country's best hope for survival. The instincts, ambition, and passion that made Franklin a successful businessman, a respected scientist, and a pivotal figure in America's struggle for freedom told him that government by consent was the only path the fledgling country could take, and that compromise and conciliation were vital to their shared future as a nation.

Benjamin Franklin died in Philadelphia on April 17, 1790.